The Vicar of Bray

The Vicar of Bray

Sydney Grundy and
Edward Solomon

MINT EDITIONS

The Vicar of Bray was first published in 1882.

This edition published by Mint Editions 2021.

ISBN 9781513281384 | E-ISBN 9781513286402

Published by Mint Editions®

MINT EDITIONS

minteditionbooks.com

Publishing Director: Jennifer Newens
Design & Production: Rachel Lopez Metzger
Project Manager: Micaela Clark
Typesetting: Westchester Publishing Services

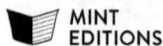

Dramatis Personae

Rev. William Barlow (Vicar of Bray)
Rev. Henry Sandford (his Curate and Pupil)
Thomas Merton, Esq. (of Bray Manor—another Pupil)
Mr. Bedford Rowe (a Confidential Family Solicitor)
John Dory   }
Peter Piper   }   (Students)
Samuel Spicer }
First Huntsman
Second Huntsman
Mrs. Merton (a Widow)
Nelly Bly (a Premiere Danseuse)
Cynthia   }
Agatha   }
Blanche   }   (Lady Teachers)
Rose   }
Gertrude   }
Winifred (the Vicar's Daughter)

Chorus of Huntsmen, Students, Lady Teachers, and Ladies of the Ballet.

Act. I.—Low Church
Scene.—The Village Green

Act II.—High Church
Scene.—The Vicarage Grounds

Act I

SCENE.—*The Village Green.*

CHORUS OF SCHOOL CHILDREN.

Hurray! hurray! hurray!
We've got a holiday!
And that is why we gaily cry,
Hurray! hurray! hurray!
ALL: Ladies and gentlemen, how do you do?
BOYS: We bring from our master a message to you.
GIRLS: Our reverend pastor instructs us to say—
BOYS: That these are the schools of the Vicar of Bray.
GIRLS: We are the children who go to the schools—
BOYS: And this annual holiday's one of the rules.
GIRLS: At skipping rope—
BOYS: Peg-top—
GIRLS: We're longing to play—
ALL: So we all of us wish you a very good day.
Hurray! hurray! hurray!
We've got a holiday!
The cat's away—the mice will play
Hurray! hurray! hurray!
Enter LADY TEACHERS.

CHORUS OF LADY TEACHERS.

To a slow and stately measure,
Walking out in single file,
Sadly do we take our pleasure,
Working slippers all the while.
Ah me! for how many preachers
Have we laboured? We forget!
We are the young lady teachers,
And we are not married yet!

       Although
They follow us methodically,
And they periodically
Squeeze our hand spasmodically—
    Tantalizing tribe!
Men who so insensible are,
And so indefensible are,
Words that are reprehensible are
    Only can describe!

Enter WINIFRED.

WINIFRED: The old refrain!

CYNTHIA, BLANCHE: The old refrain!

AGATHA: How many years have we been singing it?

WINIFRED: Ever since papa began to receive pupils to be prepared for their D.D. And he's had a good many.

CYNTHIA: Yes, they come and go.

BLANCHE: We don't.

WINIFRED: It's very discouraging, but don't lose heart.

CYNTHIA: If the Vicar changed his curate as often as his students, our prospects would be brighter; but Mr. Sandford seems to be a fixture.

WINIFRED: Fortunately, papa has him on a lease.

CHORUS: A lease!

WINIFRED: When he was quite a boy, so exemplary was his conduct, that he became my father's favourite pupil; and when he was ordained, papa determined to secure his services for a term of years.

BLANCHE: At what rent?

WINIFRED: Fifty pounds per annum.

AGATHA: It isn't very much.

WINIFRED: True! but you must remember that papa covenanted to keep him in good order and preservation, and to deliver him up on the expiration of the term in the same excellent condition in which he found him.

CYNTHIA: Then it's a repairing lease.

WINIFRED: Precisely so.

AGATHA: The Vicar must have thought very highly of him.

WINIFRED: Henry is a man after papa's heart.

BLANCHE: After yours, you mean.

AGATHA: There is no man after my heart.

CYNTHIA: She wishes there was.

                     SYDNEY GRUNDY AND EDWARD SOLOMON

BLANCHE: Cynthia! you are so unmaiden-like.

CYNTHIA: My dear, when men persist in being maiden-like, the only recourse for maidens is to be man-like.

WINIFRED: I quite agree with Cynthia.

SONG.—WINIFRED.

Oh, why is my love so cold to me?
    Oh, why is my love so blind?
His passion he long since told to me—
    Oh, can he have changed his mind?
As certain as I'm an only lass,
    I shouldn't have been so sad,
If he had been born a lonely lass
    And I had been born a lad.

TEACHERS: That's very true.

WINIFRED: What's very true?

TEACHERS: As certain as you're an only lass,
    You wouldn't have been so sad,

ALL: If he had been born a lonely lass
    And I had been born a lad.

His love for me once was strong enough—
    Oh, can it have passed away?
Alack-a-day, life's not long enough
    For dalliance and delay.
Oh! why is my love so cold to me?
    Oh, why is my love so coy?
A maiden had been more bold to me,
    If I had been born a boy.

TEACHERS: No doubt of that!

WINIFRED: No doubt of what?

TEACHERS: No doubt that your love is cold to you!
    No doubt that your love is coy!
A maiden had been more bold to you
    If you had been born a boy.

WINIFRED: Come, girls, let us join the children.

AGATHA: Even in its hours of recreation youth requires control.

BLANCHE: Besides, we may meet the students.

Exit of WINIFRED and TEACHERS.

TEACHERS: All the bold and all the bad girls
        Husbands without number get;
    We are sober, staid, and sad girls,
        And we are not married yet.
Exeunt.
Enter SANDFORD *and* STUDENTS.

CHORUS OF STUDENTS.

    On, Students, on!
        On, Students of Divinity!
    Brothers in love,
        If not in consanguinity!
SANDFORD: On, Students, on!
JOHN: Oh, stay, for we are weary!
SANDFORD: Why weary, John?
STUDENTS: The Vicar's style is dreary.
SANDFORD: (*shocked*) Oh, Students, oh!
STUDENTS: Our hapless heads are aching.
SANDFORD: So, Students, so!
STUDENTS: Besides our hearts are breaking.
SANDFORD: Fie, Students, fie!
STUDENTS: We love the lady teachers.
SANDFORD: Why, Students, why!
STUDENTS: They are our fellow creatures.
SANDFORD: And from our youth up we've been taught
        By one and all our teachers,
    That every virtuous student ought
        To love his fellow creatures.
ALL: That every virtuous student ought
        To love his fellow creatures.

SANDFORD: My friends, let us not dwell on this distressing theme;
    I have much to say to you.
JOHN: Yes, Harry, you generally have.
SANDFORD: I wish to unbosom myself to you on a subject which has
    for years occasioned me the greatest distress and consternation. I
    allude to the melancholy deterioration in the moral character of my
    old friend and tutor, Mr. Barlow.

SAMUEL: What's the matter with him?

PETER: I like him well enough.

JOHN: Out of the lecture-room.

SANDFORD: Ever since he was inducted into the Vicarage of Bray, he has been a changed man. Not only have the flowing periods in which he was wont to indulge given place to a colloquial diction, but that lamentable latitudinarianism which is traditionally associated with the living, appears to have penetrated his intellectual and spiritual nature. He is now Low Church.

JOHN: Well, so are you.

SANDFORD: I was always Low—so was Mr. Barlow originally; but when he became Vicar of Bray, he became Broad—very Broad—shockingly Broad. Then he turned Low again, and married the late Mrs. Eleanor Ann Barlow. I am unable to shut my eyes to the fact that the late Mrs. Barlow was also Low.

JOHN: She had a little money, hadn't she?

SANDFORD: That is the painful part of the case. Distressing as it is—

PETER: Oh, I say, Harry! (*Yawns*)

SANDFORD: I cannot shut my eyes—

SAMUEL: And we can scarcely keep ours open.

JOHN: We've had one lecture this morning.

SAMUEL: Give us a song.

SANDFORD: It always affords me pleasure to accede to requests with which it is in my power to comply. I will give you a song.

SONG.—SANDFORD, WITH CHORUS OF STUDENTS.

When I was a Sunday-school scholar,
　　I was an example to boys,
For I never rumpled my collar,
　　And I never made any noise;
I never spoke words out of season,
　　I never did anything wrong,
And that, I've no doubt, is the reason
　　My youth was as happy as long.
Ah, why was it happy? because
　　A better boy never was seen;
I was not only as good as I was,
　　But as good as I ought to have been!

STUDENTS: Ah, why was he happy? etc.
    I grew up to manhood's estate,
        Without having told an untruth;
    I practise, I'm proud to relate,
        The precepts I learnt in my youth.
    I carry them out to the letter,
        I'm really as good as a book;
    Indeed I am very much better;
        In fact, I'm as good as I look!
    I revel in pastry and jam,
        I'm a terrible topper at tea;
    I am not only as good as I am,
        But as good as I ought to be!
STUDENTS: You may tell by the look of his phiz
        He revels in toffee and tea;
    For he is not only as good as he is,
        But as good as he ought to be!
(*The following verse appears in the vocal score but not in the libretto*)
    In me is a living example,
        Of what you should be if you can,
    I hope you will all take a sample
        Of perhaps a phenomenal man;
    For if you don't pay me attention
        You'll come to a very bad end.
    And lastly I may as well mention
        It's never too late to amend.
    Abandon the pipe and cigar
        And drink nothing stronger than tea
    You'll be not only as good as you are,
        But as good as you ought to be!
STUDENTS: Abandon the pipe and cigar, etc.
Re-enter OMNES.

ENSEMBLE.—WINIFRED, VICAR, CHILDREN, TEACHERS,
AND STUDENTS.

CHILDREN: Hurray! hurray! hurray!
    The Vicar comes this way!
        That's why we trip and hop and skip,

And hop and skip along!
    Hurray! hurray! hurray!
        He's promised us a song!
        That's why we say, hurray! hurray!
        And may his life be long!
WINIFRED: Here comes Papa!
    Hurrah! hurrah! hurrah!
TEACHERS: Now let us give him greeting!
CHILDREN: The first of May
    It is today—
ALL: So this is a May meeting.
    Uniting our voices this morning
        All hail to the Vicar of Bray!

Enter VICAR.

CHILDREN: Long live he, his office adorning—
    His humble parishoners pray!
TEACHERS: We teachers, we send to him greeting!
CHILDREN: We children, who go to his school!
TEACHERS: We members of his Dorcas meeting!
STUDENTS: We students who're under his rule.
VICAR: My brethren, as swelleth the ocean,
    So swelleth my bosom today.
CHILDREN: He cannot control his emotion!
ALL: All hail to the Vicar of Bray!
SANDFORD: (*advancing*) Mr. Barlow, it has been publicly announced
    that it is your intention to oblige the company with a comic song.
VICAR: I've promised to tell the children how I came to be Vicar of Bray.
SANDFORD: Sir, I would seriously ask you to reconsider your determination.
VICAR: Certainly not.
SANDFORD: Then I will withdraw.
WINIFRED: (*approaching him*) Henry, I may not agree with you—I may
    even regard your scruples as Quixotic—but I will accompany you.

Exeunt SANDFORD *and* WINIFRED.

JOHN: That young man gives himself airs.
VICAR: And yet he objects to my giving you one. I must admit, the
    song is scarcely of a sacerdotal character, but "Non semper tendit
    acrum Apollo," eh, Spicer?
STUDENTS: Ha! ha! ha!
VICAR: This is the first of May, and I will unbend.

Song.—Vicar.

Your Sandford and Merton you've read, I suppose?
It's a story that every little boy knows—
How Tommy was wealthy and Tommy was bad;
And Henry, he was an exemplary lad;
Their tutor you haven't forgotten, I'm sure;
His style was didactic, his manner demure,
Of language he had a magnificent flow,
And his name was the Reverend Mister Barlow.

Chorus: His name was the Reverend Mister Barlow.

In Jamaica the scene of the story was laid,
Where the father of Thomas made money by trade,
But a fever soon carried off Tommy's papa,
And Tommy came over here with his mama.
His clerical teacher was in the same boat,
And the excellent Henry was also afloat;
The passage was rough, and I happen to know,
Very ill was the Reverend Mister Barlow.

Chorus: Very ill was the Reverend Mister Barlow.

Together they landed in England one day,
And they all settled down in the village of Bray,
For there Mrs. Merton, I ought to remark,
Had a beautiful mansion, and also a park.
What is more to the point, in her patronage lay
The gift of the snug little living of Bray,
And into it she, her good feeling to shew,
Inducted the Reverend Mr. Barlow.

Chorus: Inducted the Reverend Mr. Barlow.

(*The following verse appears in the vocal score but not in the libretto*)

Now Henry's the Curate, and Tommy's the Squire,
What more can their Reverend tutor desire?
Except to be Master—albeit a Clerk—
Of the beautiful mansion and also the park;
To marry his daughter to Tommy the bad,
Instead of to Henry, the excellent lad;
For between you and me, but no further to go,
An eye to the main chance has Mr. Barlow.

Chorus: An eye to the main chance has Mr. Barlow.

SYDNEY GRUNDY AND EDWARD SOLOMON

Re-enter SANDFORD.

VICAR: Here again, Henry?

SANDFORD: I want to speak to you seriously.

VICAR: You always do. I wish to goodness you wouldn't.

SANDFORD: I will make no further allusion to the unseemly song of which the frivolous refrain still echoes in my ears.

VICAR: Henry, your rounded periods irritate me. Do talk rationally.

SANDFORD: It is you, Mr. Barlow, who are responsible for the rotundity of my periods. Was it not you who instructed me?

VICAR: You were a babe then, and I gave you milk for babes. Now that you are a man, you ought to have more common sense.

SANDFORD: Sir, I would ask you seriously to reflect whether common sense in conjunction with rectitude can reasonably be expected for fifty pounds per annum.

VICAR: Well, perhaps not.

SANDFORD: And that brings me to the point; I want to apply to you for an augmentation of my stipend.

VICAR: You forget, Mr. Sandford, that I have you on a lease.

SANDFORD: It is too true. You took advantage of my ignorance of the market value of my noble qualities to secure the exclusive enjoyment of them for a term of years. But inasmuch as I am about to become your son—

VICAR: My son!

SANDFORD: Winifred has just accepted me.

VICAR: Look here, Sandford, I've put up with you and your rounded periods long enough. I give you a month's notice. You can look for another curacy.

SANDFORD: You forget, Mr. Barlow, that the term of our indenture has not yet expired.

VICAR: At least, I can refuse to sanction your engagement to Winifred. I have other views for her.

SANDFORD: You allude to my old fellow pupil, Tommy Merton.

VICAR: Never mind what I allude to.

SANDFORD: Mr. Barlow, I have long been a melancholy witness of your moral degeneration, but never—

VICAR: Don't lecture me, sir.

SANDFORD: You lectured me enough in my youth, and it is only right that I should return the obligation. Bruised reed that I am—

VICAR: Go, sir—go, without further argument.

SANDFORD: Sir, I will go—I go in tribulation.

VICAR: You may go in what you like, sir.

SANDFORD: But remember, you have broken my heart. This is a distinct breach of covenant. I shall at once have my injuries assessed by a sworn appraiser, and tomorrow you will hear from my solicitor. (*Exit*)

VICAR: From his solicitor! As if a man on fifty pounds a year can possibly afford a solicitor! I must consult Rowe about this. Ah! here he comes! (*Goes up*)

CHORUS.—CHILDREN, TEACHERS, AND STUDENTS.

STUDENTS: Bow! Students, bow!

TEACHERS: And ladies, curtsey low!

CHILDREN: Bob! children, bob!

ALL: To Mister Bedford Rowe!

STUDENTS: Whilst some are gentlemen by birth,
        And some are so by station,

TEACHERS: What others are by rank and worth,
        He is by Legislation.

CHILDREN: The justice and the common sense
        Of this we never saw.

ALL: Still let us humbly reverence
        The majesty of law!

Bow! Students, bow! etc.

Enter MR. BEDFORD ROWE.

SONG.—BEDFORD ROWE and CHORUS
(CHILDREN, TEACHERS, and STUDENTS).

I'm as sharp as a ferret;
    From dad I inherit
A legal and logical mind;
    I'm as clever and comely
    As Lumley and Lumley
And Lewis and Lewis combined.
    Yield to Lickfold I don't, nor
    To Wontner and Wontner;

SYDNEY GRUNDY AND EDWARD SOLOMON

I'm even with Bolton and Mote;
> You have no need to call
> On Freke Palmer at all—

I can row in the very same boat.

CHORUS: You have no need to call, etc.

ROWE: "Now, witness, remember, you are on your oath—answer me, aye or no, were you drunk on the occasion in question?" "Well, it depends on what you call drunk!" "Never mind what I call drunk, sir? Answer me, aye or no?" "Well, I'd had a glass!" "Only one glass, sir?" "Aye." "Yes, you, sir, you!" "Aye!" "Answer my question, sir!" "I've answered it." "No, sir; you asked another. You said 'I?'" "Well, you told me to say aye or no." "Really, m'lud, in the course of my professional experience—" (*resumes seat*)

ROWE: A witness I'll bustle
> As well as Charles Russell,

Sir Edward I equal in skill.
> I'm a Lockwood at larks
> And at hitting my marks

I'm a second edition of Gill.

CHORUS: He's a Lockwood at larks, etc.

ROWE: But when one fine morning
> The bench I'm adorning—

And one day I mean to be there—
> You will find, all the knowledge
> I've learnt in life's college

Has disappeared into thin air.
> In my ignorance crass
> I shall be such an ass,

The grass itself won't be as green;
> In my innocence—well,
> I shall fairly excel

Mister Gilbert's young maid of fifteen!

CHORUS: In his innocence, etc.

ROWE: "Spoof? What is spoof?" "Spoof, m'lud, is a slang term, signifying"—"Slang! what is slang?" "Slang, m'lud, is a sort of spoken shorthand, compressing the greatest possible quantity of meaning into the smallest possible quantity of words—a summing-up, in fact, m'lud." "I do not find any mention of the word, 'spoof,' in Johnson's Dictionary." "No, m'lud, the word is not to be found in

Johnson, I admit." "If your ludship pleases, may I, as amicus curiae, be permitted to explain that 'spoof' is the name colloquially applied to the game that lawyers play with their clients." "Oh, thank you, Mr. Lockwood—now I understand." "If y'ludship pleases."

Rowe: But about my pretense
        Of supreme innocence
    There'll be just a suspicion of fudge
        For the baby unborn
        Is not such a greenhorn
    As the octogenarian judge!

Chorus: For the baby unborn, etc.

Vicar: And now, my young friends, I must ask you to leave me for a few moments, as I have important business with my confidential family solicitor.

Chorus: Good morning, dear Vicar, good morning.

Exeunt Chorus.

Rowe: You sent for me!

Vicar: Yes, Rowe! I want to consult you generally as to my affairs. Firstly, as you are aware, I have some thoughts of marrying Mrs. Merton. She is a widow—I am a widower.

Rowe: She has money—you have none.

Vicar: Precisely! Rowe, what I like about you is your happy knack of coming to the point without any circumlocution. You are the confidential family solicitor of the late Thomas Merton.

Rowe: Formerly of Jamaica, sugar planter. I was.

Vicar: What I want to know is, does or does not Mrs. Merton's property revert to her late husband's estate in the event of her re-marriage?

Rowe: It does not.

Vicar: You're quite sure?

Rowe: Drew the will myself.

Vicar: Good! Secondly, I wish to marry Winifred to Tommy Merton.

Rowe: Capital match! You couldn't do better!

Vicar: Unfortunately, Tommy has set his affections on the premiere danseuse of the corps de ballet of the Theatre Royal—a notorious young person—

Rowe: Nelly Bly!

Vicar: You know her?

Rowe: I am her confidential family solicitor.

VICAR: To make matters worse, Winifred has taken it into her head to fall in love with my curate. You know Sandford?

ROWE: I am his confidential family solicitor.

VICAR: Rowe, what I like about you is, that you're everybody's solicitor! You must know I have Sandford for a term of years.

ROWE: Didn't I draft the indenture myself?

VICAR: So you did! Consequently I can't give him notice; and yet I can do nothing to bring matters between Winifred and Tommy to a head whilst he is in the neighbourhood.

ROWE: You want me to get rid of him?

VICAR: Rowe, your happy knack of coming to the point is truly wonderful.

ROWE: It's the simplest thing in the world. Sandford is conscientious. He is a prig, but he is a conscientious prig.

VICAR: Rowe, your happy knack of calling a spade a spade—

ROWE: He is Low Church.

VICAR: He is.

ROWE: You are also Low Church?

VICAR: I am.

ROWE: But you are a time-server.

VICAR: Rowe, your offensive habit of calling a spade a spade—

ROWE: I speak as between attorney and client. Turn High Church.

VICAR: What then?

ROWE: Sandford will of his own accord resign his curacy.

VICAR: A capital idea! My dear Rowe, you're an ornament to your profession.

ROWE: My dear Barlow, we're a pair of ornaments.

MRS. MERTON (*without*).

Has anyone seen the Pytchley pack?
    Has anyone met the Quorn?
Or a handsome youth on a horse's back,
    Who carries a bugle horn?

VICAR: The widow, I declare!

Enter MRS. MERTON.

MRS. M.: Good morning, gentlemen.

VICAR: My dear Mrs. Merton!

MRS. M.: Have you seen Tommy? I feel sure some dreadful accident has happened. He will go out hunting, and he doesn't know how.

Rowe: Hunting in May!

Mrs. M.: It doesn't matter what the season is, it's all the same to him.

Vicar: Your son was always fond of having his own way.

Mrs. M.: Ah, Mr. Barlow!

Vicar: Ah, Mrs. Merton!

Mrs. M.: If he'd only settle down! If he'd marry Winifred!

Vicar: Ah, Mrs. Merton!

Mrs. M.: Ah, Mr. Barlow!

Rowe: Excuse me for interrupting you. You wish your son to marry Mr. Barlow's daughter. Why not make him?

Mrs. M.: How?

Rowe: Simplest thing in the world. You have a general power of appointment over your late husband's estate. Threaten to disinherit him.

Mrs. M.: A happy thought! How can I thank you?

Vicar: Rowe, as a confidential family solicitor, I don't know your equal.

Trio.—Mrs. Merton, Vicar, and Rowe.

Rowe: Now, if you'll excuse me, I'll wish you good day
　　I've a sort of a feeling that I'm in the way.

Mrs. M.: Oh, dear me, no!

Vicar: Not a bit of it, Rowe.

Rowe: I am perfectly certain that I am de trop.

Vicar: Oh, Bedford, what nonsense! now, don't run away!

Mrs. M.: My dear Mr. Rowe, I implore you to stay.

Rowe: Oh, dear me, no, I had much rather go.
　　It is perfectly evident I am de trop.

Ensemble.

Rowe: It is perfectly evident I am de trop.

Mrs. M.: For goodness sake, don't be absurd, Mr. Rowe.

Vicar: There isn't the slightest occasion to go.

Exit Rowe.

Vicar: We are alone! the lawyer's gone at last!

Mrs. M.: We are alone! Why beats my heart so fast?

　　　　SYDNEY GRUNDY AND EDWARD SOLOMON

Duet.—Mrs. Merton and Vicar.

VICAR: My dear Mistress Merton, pray cease these alarms!
    My reverend office suspicion disarms.
    This coyness is prompted by excellent taste,
    But neither of us has a moment to waste,
    So don't shilly-shally, but wed while you can!
MRS. M.: Go along with you, will you, you obstinate man!
VICAR: Oh, walk in the footsteps of Eleanor Ann!
MRS. M.: You know very well you've been married before,
    And the late Mistress Barlow had beauty galore,
    Whatever, such being the case, can you see
    To admire in a middle-aged widow like me?
VICAR: The late Mistress Barlow was nothing to you,
MRS. M.: Oh, you obstinate man, go along with you, do,
VICAR: Oh, put yourself into Ann Eleanor's shoe.
VICAR: Matilda, enough of this excellent taste,
    And let me encircle that matronly waist!
    Remember the time will be soon out of joint,
    So don't shilly-shally, but come to the point!
    Oh, come to the arms that are waiting for you!
MRS. M.: Oh, you excellent man, I don't mind if I do,
VICAR: Well, I'm sure that is quite the best thing you can do.
They dance off.
Re-enter WINIFRED *and* SANDFORD
WINIFRED: You've spoken to papa?
SANDFORD: And he refuses to accord his sanction to our betrothal; but
    this trifling circumstance does not alter my determination to make
    you my wife.
WINIFRED (*embracing him*): Dearest!
SANDFORD (*withdrawing, shocked*): We are not married yet, Winifred,
    and I cannot conscientiously permit demonstrations of affection
    which have not received the sanction of a civil and religious
    ceremony.
WINIFRED: Harry!
SANDFORD: My name is Henry; and the familiar contraction of my
    baptismal appellation is painfully suggestive of theatrical and
    sporting publications of a pernicious character.
WINIFRED: How happy we shall be together!

SANDFORD: You are indeed a fortunate woman. All that Nuttall's
   Dictionary can do to make you happy, shall be done.
WINIFRED: But Harry—Henry! A dreadful thought occurs to me! Are
   you your own to give away?
SANDFORD: It is true that your father held me for a term which
   has yet some years to run; but he has repudiated his covenants,
   so I have re-entered and determined the lease.
WINIFRED: But, in that case, what shall we live upon?
SANDFORD: There is a considerable sum due for dilapidations.
WINIFRED (*about to embrace him again*): Harry!
SANDFORD (*putting her aside*): Winifred, I cannot allow it. The utmost
   that I can permit you to do is join me in a duet—which I have
   desired the composer to arrange in such a fashion that I shall
   appear to greater advantage than you.

DUET.—WINIFRED AND SANDFORD.

SANDFORD: Tell me, and oh tell me true, love,
   Will thy heart be ever mine?
Tell me, will those eyes of blue, love,
   Ever on my path-way shine?
Life is not a marriage measure;
   Though our spirits bound awhile,
Love is pain as well as pleasure,
   And must weep as well as smile;

ENSEMBLE.

SANDFORD: Tell me, and oh tell me true, love,
   With thy blue eyes fixed on mine,
Naught shall come between us two, love—
   Come between my heart and thine!
WINIFRED: Yes, I'll tell thee, tell thee true, love,
   With my blue eyes fixed on thine,
Naught shall come between us two, love—
   Come between thy heart and mine!
WINIFRED: Yes, I tell thee, tell thee true, love,
   Thou art mine and I am thine!
Look into mine eyes of blue, love,

And my inmost heart divine.
She who loveth, loveth ever,
    Through the sunshine, through the rain,
Loveth on without endeavour.
    Though her heart be only pain.

Ensemble.

SANDFORD: Tell me, and oh tell me true, love, etc.
WINIFRED: Yes, I'll tell thee, tell thee true, love, etc.
Exeunt.
Enter CHORUS *of* HUNTSMEN, *led by* TOMMY MERTON.

Chorus of Huntsmen.

Jolly, jolly huntsmen, huntsmen we!
You should see us riding 'cross countree!
Hunting with the Pytchley, hunting with the Quorn,
Yoiks, tally-ho, boys! sound the bugle horn!

Solo.—Tommy Merton.

Our chorus is somewhat peculiar
    Perhaps you've not heard it before,
But if you won't think we unruly are,
    We'll presently give you some more.
To tell the truth of the matter
    We're none of us huntsmen at all,
We only create a great clatter
    And hulloa and halloa and bawl.
(*The following verse appears in the vocal score but not in the libretto*)
    We join in the meet and view hallo
        And then we are prudently dumb
    For if we attempted to follow
        To grief we should certainly come.
    Although as fox hunters we're painted
        Our portraits are hanging at home
    The brush with which we are acquainted
        Is that which is used with a comb.

We purchased these picturesque raiments,
    Though there no more huntsmen than earls,
(And settle by quarterly payments)
    Because it goes down with the girls.
We flatter ourselves, our collective
    Appearance is rather the thing;
The bugle horn's very effective,
    And that's why we halloa and sing.

HUNTSMEN: Jolly, jolly huntsmen, huntsmen we! etc.

TOMMY (*mopping his forehead*): Phew! This is very hard work!

1ST HUNTSMAN: And no girls to hear us.

TOMMY: Not yet, but they'll be here directly.

2ND HUNTSMAN: Who?

TOMMY: Nelly Bly and the Corps de Ballet.

1ST HUNTSMAN: Here?

2ND HUNTSMAN: At the Vicarage?

TOMMY: The Corps de Ballet of the Theatre Royal, horror-struck by the schisms and dissensions in the Church, have formed themselves into a Co-operative Clerical Reform Association, and they are coming to interview the Vicar. Here they are.

Enter CORPS DE BALLET.

CHORUS and SOLOS.—AGATHA and CYNTHIA
and CORPS DE BALLET.
CORPS DE BALLET.

Please to make way for us, please to make way!
Way for a Terpsichorean display!
Don't be alarmed, we are clothed to the feet
In a becoming accordion pleat!

CYNTHIA: Into place sliding,
    Gracefully gliding,
Eyeing the house with a languid eye,
    Soberly setting,
    And pirouetting
Oh, did you ever see maids so shy?

AGATHA: Petticoats twinkling,
    Give me but an inkling,
    Modest and mystic, of ankles and feet;

BOTH: Flounces ad libit,
　　Is all we exhibit
　　Under the modern accordion pleat.
ALL: Petticoats twinkling, etc.
Enter NELLY BLY.

DANCE.

Re-enter OMNES.

CHORUS—TEACHERS AND STUDENTS.

　　Oh! shocking sight to met a pious eye!
　　Speak, someone speak! this scandal justify!
VICAR: Surely I know some of these young ladies?
AGATHA: Yes, Vicar, I used to be one of your lady teachers.
CYNTHIA: And I.
BLANCHE: And I.
VICAR: I thought I recognised you. You have left the Sunday
　　school?
CYNTHIA: Well, of course, we only joined the Sunday school to try
　　and get husbands.
BLANCHE: And we tried hard.
VICAR: You did—you did. I observed your efforts.
AGATHA: But they failed.
CYNTHIA: So we went on the stage.
VICAR: And very nice you look in your new dresses. But bless me! I
　　was under the impression that on the stage young ladies wore—
　　mind you, I have not seen them—I have only seen pictures.
NELLY: Pictures of what?
VICAR: Well, of this sort of thing.
NELLY: Ah, that was before the invention of the convoluted skirt.
　　Nowadays we leave "that sort of thing" to the bishops.
VICAR: Who is this young person?
NELLY: Nelly Bly, your reverence.
VICAR: The name sounds familiar. Is it possible that you are the young
　　lady who, on a memorable occasion, shut her eye?
NELLY: Yes, I was very young then. It's been opened since.
VICAR: I am delighted to meet you; but what brings you here?

NELLY: The ladies of the corps de ballet have come to invite you to a tea party which they are about to give to the clergy of the surrounding parishes. There will be cakes and buns, after which we shall address you.

VICAR: You will address the clergy?

NELLY: Why not? You're always trying to improve us; why shouldn't we try to improve you? I come to hear you preach twice a week, but you never come to see me dance. I don't call that fair.

VICAR: It is not fair. There is a great deal of common sense in this young lady's observations.

SANDFORD: If I might be allowed, I should like to say a few words.

VICAR: No doubt, Henry; it wouldn't be you if you didn't want to say a good many.

SANDFORD: I would suggest that these young persons be requested to withdraw; the baleful influence of their presence is already only too apparent.

FINALE OF ACT I.

SANDFORD: Back, students, back,
    Cast not these side-long glances!
STUDENTS (*to* BALLET): Sisters in love!
TEACHERS (*to* STUDENTS): They are not your fiancees!
VICAR: Stay, Sandford, stay!
    And hear me make confession!
  What I have heard today
    Has made a deep impression!

I'm Low at present, no one Lower—
    But now, Low Church, good-bye!
I mean to be a theatre-goer,
    And generally, generally High!
ALL: And generally, generally High!
CHILDREN: Hurray! hurray! hurray!
BALLET, STUDENTS, and HUNTSMEN: Hurray! for Nelly Bly!
SANDFORD: Alack the day!
CHILDREN: Hurray! hurray!
ALL: He's going to be High!
VICAR: Henceforth, I proclaim a vendetta

Against Evangelical ways;
In a chasuble and a biretta
The wrath of my bishop I'll raise!
I was always a bit of a sham!
Consistency's nothing to me!
So I'll be no longer Low as I am,
But as High as I oughtn't to be!

ALL: What terrible language is this?
He says we shall presently see
That he'll be no longer as Low as he is
But as High as he oughtn't to be!

ROWE: Great is my learning and research
In all pertaining to the church—
I'll just give you a sample!

ALL: He'll just give us a sample!

ROWE: Whatever Mr. Barlow be—
Or High or Low, it's clear to me
His students of divinity
Must follow his example.

VICAR: Not a doubt of it, Rowe, that is certainly so.

MRS. M.: To argue the matter is really de trop.

ALL: To argue the matter is really de trop.

SANDFORD: I, rather than infringe the law,
To foreign climes will go;
The Casowary and Choctaw
Shall cheer me in my woe.

WINIFRED: Oh, do not leave me,
Do not leave me so.

CHORUS: Do not leave her so.

WINIFRED: Speak to me, Henry
Say why need you go.

CHORUS: Say why need you go.

SANDFORD: 'Tis duty calls me hence, I must not stay.

CHORUS: He must obey

WINIFRED: If duty calls you, then you must not stay.

ALL: Heroic girl!

ROWE: (*to* VICAR) This is your own contriving!

VICAR: I can't make out at what on earth you're driving.

SANDFORD: Farewell, students!

STUDENTS: Farewell, Henry!

SANDFORD: Grief of mine no words can tell.

CHILDREN: Farewell, Henry!

SANDFORD: Farewell, children!
 I can only say farewell!

ALL: Farewell!

Exit SANDFORD

VICAR: But whither tends your argument?
 I fail to see to what extent
  Your premises you carry.

ROWE: All being High, I beg to state
 It will be your untoward fate
 For ever to be celibate,
  So none of you can marry.

ALL: Oh! horror! misery! despair!
  However long we/they tarry
 The thought is more than we/they can bear!
  We/They none of us/them can marry!

End of Act I.

Twelve Months Elapse.

Act II

SCENE.—*The Vicarage Grounds.*

CHORUS OF LADY TEACHERS.

Listen to the merry music of the bells,
  Wedding bells, wedding bells,
  Sweet is the tale it tells!
Now it coyly carols—now it soars and swells,
Singing their madrigal, list to the bells!
    Chiming, chiming!
Ringing out cheerily, "Sigh not so wearily,
  Though sorrow smite you again and again,"
Carolling merrily, telling us verily
  Life has its pleasure as well as its pain!

ROSE: What a change in our prospects!

GERTRUDE: I can scarcely believe it! Suppose it should turn out to be all a dream!

CHORUS: Oh, Gertrude!

ROSE: I have consulted Mr. Bedford Rowe, my confidential family solicitor.

CHORUS: So have I!

ROSE: And he assures me that our engagements to the huntsmen are absolute and indefeasible. What fine fellows they are!

GERTRUDE: How picturesque their costume!

ROSE: How manly—how thoroughly English in their devotion to the chase. Out every day, regardless of the weather.

GERTRUDE: Or the season.

The Students' symphony is heard in the distance.

ROSE: Here come those stupid students!

GERTRUDE: To their morning lecture.

CHORUS: We won't speak to them!

All walk aside.

Enter STUDENTS.

CONCERTED PIECE.—STUDENTS, TEACHERS, and VICAR.

STUDENTS: What is life? a dreary desert; hapless, hopeless,
pilgrims we,
Doomed for ever and for ever to celibacy!
Cruel maids, we stand before you,
Broken-hearted, bruised men;
Knowing well how we adore you,
Will you not adore again?

TEACHERS: You robbed us of our peace of mind,
The Huntsmen have restored it.

STUDENTS: We'll marry you, if you'll be kind.

TEACHERS: Oh, no, you can't afford it!

Exit TEACHERS.

STUDENTS: Single ever, married never, piteous is our fate!

Enter VICAR.

VICAR: Life is a Gregorian measure long and desolate!

VICAR: I must admit that when I became a pervert, I did not
foresee all that it involved; but let me point out that there are
compensating advantages. Firstly, we have got rid of Sandford.

JOHN: Poor Harry!

PETER: Has nothing more been heard of him?

VICAR: Since the discovery of his hymn-book amongst the remains
of a cannibalistic festival, not a word. It is only too obvious that
although we couldn't swallow him, the Casowaries have found him
more to their taste.

CHORUS: Poor Harry!

VICAR: Secondly, it cannot be denied that in my new vestments I
present an imposing appearance. I not only look imposing—

CHORUS: You are imposing!

VICAR: Thirdly and lastly, we are now regular attendants at the theatre,
and also at the instructive and fascinating five o'clock tea parties of
the ladies of the corps de ballet.

CHORUS: Hear! hear!

VICAR: Gentlemen, inasmuch as my dear daughter, Winifred, is
about to gladden my heart in marrying this morning my esteemed
and opulent old pupil, Tommy Merton, my lecture to-day will
be remarkable chiefly for its brevity. Its subject will be "The
Institution of Matrimony."

SYDNEY GRUNDY AND EDWARD SOLOMON

Song.—Vicar and Chorus of Students.

Vicar: A maiden who marries, her steps may retrace—
Students: Pa-ce the Jackson case!
Vicar: She may kick up her heels up all over the place
Students: Vide the Jackson case!
Vicar: A husband's no longer a right to the wife—
Students: E.g. the Jackson case!
Vicar: But still he is bound to support her for life
Students: Good, good old Jackson case!
Vicar: The old superstition,
   That wives have a mission,
     Is slapped in the face—
Students: By the Jackson case!
Vicar: But mark you, a bridegroom has just the same grace—
Students: N.B. the Jackson case!
Vicar: A husband may also kick over the trace—
Students: Pa-ce the Jackson case!
Vicar: A man and a woman are married for life—
Students: E.g. the Jackson case!
Vicar: But a husband's not bound to go home with his wife!
Students: Good, good old Jackson case!
Vicar: The female opinion,
   That man is a minion
     Is slapped in the face—
Students: By the Jackson case!
Vicar: The Jackson decision is excellent law.
Students: Good law, the Jackson case!
Vicar: And if anybody's inclined to say "pshaw!"
Students: "Pooh! Pooh! the Jackson case!"
Vicar: The reason is simply they don't understand
Students: Either the Jackson case.—
Vicar: Or what has been always the law of the land—
Students: I.e. the Jackson case!
Vicar: A prevalent error,
   That wedlock's a terror
     Is slapped in the face—
Students: By the Jackson case!
Exeunt Students.

Enter WINIFRED.

VICAR: Winifred!

WINIFRED: Yes, father?

VICAR: I'm surprised at you. You are about to be married to the most eligible young man in my congregation, and yet you persist in wandering about in an aimless and disconsolate manner distressing to behold.

WINIFRED: I hate Tommy Merton!

VICAR: Pooh, pooh!

WINIFRED: I love Henry.

VICAR: Tommy is rich, Tommy is rollicking!

WINIFRED: Henry was true, Henry was tender!

VICAR: Tender! Well, let's hope the Casowaries found him so!

WINIFRED: How can you jest on such a subject? Here is his hymn-book, forwarded by the British Consul per book post. See, it is scorched.

VICAR: Think no more of him; he has been devoured.

WINIFRED: I cannot wonder at the Casowaries. I could have eaten him myself. But it is very hard!

VICAR: The hymn-book? Yes, they evidently found that indigestible.

WINIFRED: Father!

VICAR: Now no expostulation! Haven't I annoyances enough? Here is my Bishop plaguing me to death with prohibitions and remonstrances against my ritualistic practices. And to add insult to injury, he is acting under the advice of Mr. Bedford Rowe, my own confidential family solicitor.

WINIFRED: But you forget, he is the Bishop's family solicitor as well.

VICAR: That's what I dislike about Rowe. He's everybody's solicitor.

Enter MRS. MERTON.

WINIFRED: Oh, father, why did you turn High? The Low are so much happier than the High!

VICAR: Why? To get rid of Sandford. But my conscience sometimes pricks me. I've a great mind to turn Low again and marry Mrs. Merton.

MRS. M.: (*aside*) He'd marry me. (*Advances*)

WINIFRED *goes up.*

MRS. M.: When shall it be?

VICAR: (*aside*) The Widow here! Oh, dear!

DUET.—MRS. MERTON AND VICAR.

MRS. M.: Dearest Vicar, tell me why
    Have you grown so cold and shy?
    Why have you so altered, why?
VICAR: 'Cause I'm High, ma'am, 'cause I'm High!
    Married we can never be;
    You must not make love to me.
    Such a course, you surely see,
    Outrages propriety.
MRS. M.: Oh, oh, oh, oh, oh, oh, oh!
VICAR: Don't exclaim so, so!
MRS. M.: Will you not turn Low, Low, Low?
VICAR: No, I tell you, no, no, no!
VICAR: Madam, I regret to say
    That I can no longer stay.
MRS. M.: William, do not go away.
VICAR: Moderate your ardour, pray,
    If you have connubial views,
    Try the Matrimonial News!
MRS. M.: I have neither time to lose,
    Time to pick, nor time to choose.
VICAR: No, I tell you, madam, no!
MRS. M.: Oh, oh, oh, oh, oh, oh, oh!
VICAR: I must really go, go, go.
MRS. M.: Do not leave me so, so, so!
Exit VICAR.
MRS. MERTON *sinks, weeping, to the ground.*
Enter TOMMY *and* CHORUS *of* HUNTSMEN.
TOMMY: (*raising her*) Good gracious! It's my mother!
CHORUS: Mrs. Merton! (*She sobs*)
TOMMY: And dissolved in tears! What is the matter? Why do you sob?
    (*She sighs*)
1ST HUNTSMAN: Why do you sigh?
TOMMY: Tell me, and tell these gentlemen.
MRS. M.: I will! (*wiping her eyes*)

SONG.—MRS. MERTON, with TOMMY and
CHORUS of HUNTSMEN.

MRS. M.: You ask me why
    I sob and sigh;
      The reason's plain,
    And so am I—
        Worse luck!
      I try in vain
      To find a swain;
    For widowed men
    Won't wed again—
        No pluck!
    I am a widow at thirty-three
    And that's what's the matter, the matter with me!
TOMMY: She is a widow of fifty, sir.
CHORUS: And that's what's the matter, the matter with her!
MRS. M.: What can I do
      But pipe my eye?
    For I am too
      Robust to die—
        You see!
    In such a pass,
      What can I say
    Except, "alas,
      Alack-a-day!
        Ah, me!"
    I am a widow at thirty-three, etc.
MRS. M.: Shall I despair
    And rent a flat,
    And cherish there
    An orphan cat?
      Not I!
    At some fair youth
      Who hath not yet
    Cut wisdom's tooth,
      My cap I'll set!
      I'll try!
    Who'd be a widow at thirty-three?

SYDNEY GRUNDY AND EDWARD SOLOMON

And if people chatter, what matter to me?
TOMMY: For every Madam there's sure a Sir—
MRS. M.: And if people chatter

    Well, what does it matter,

    Well, what does it matter, it matter to me!
CHORUS: Well, what does it matter, it matter to her!
Dance off.

WINIFRED *comes down.*

WINIFRED: Ah, what a loss is mine! Once there were moments when
    I thought Henry a trifle too particular, even pedantic! but now my
    eyes are opened to his true worth. Who else will whisper sweet
    nothings in my ear in so correct and elegant a style? But I must not
    give way. I must remember I am another's, I must forget I ever was
    his.

DUET.—WINIFRED and SANDFORD.

WINIFRED: Full well I know for evermore

    My love is lost to me;

  And yet my heart is on the shore,

    My eyes are on the sea;

  And still a grief I cannot crush

    Burns in me like a flame;

  And yet a voice I cannot hush

    Keeps calling on his name!

  Forever crying out in vain

    Across the sighing sea,

  Oh, my lost love, come back again,

    Come back again to me!
SANDFORD (*without*): Come back again to thee!

  No, not in vain!
WINIFRED: No, not in vain!

    Oh wondrous power of prayer!

  I seem to hear his voice again.
SANDFORD (*without*): Where is my darling, where?
WINIFRED: Ah, me! how real fancies seem!
SANDFORD (*without*): He has come back again to thee.
WINIFRED: It is no dream!
SANDFORD: It is no dream!

Enter SANDFORD.

BOTH: It is reality!

> I called upon his/her name, and lo!
>> Across the sighing sea,
> My own lost love of long ago!
>> Thou hast/I have come back to me/thee.

WINIFRED: Then you have not been eaten?

SANDFORD: Good gracious, no! What put such an idea in your head?

WINIFRED: This hymn-book, which was found amongst the remains of a cannibalistic festival.

SANDFORD: The remains of a Casowary bonfire.

WINIFRED: But why did you not answer my letters?

SANDFORD: I never received them!

WINIFRED: That explains everything. But, Henry, how you've altered. What has wrought this change?

SANDFORD: Travel, my dear; at home I studied only copybooks— abroad, I studied men. I went out to convert the Casowaries: they taught me, I was sadly in need of conversion myself.

WINIFRED: How did you get on with them?

SANDFORD: First rate! I found the King a very jolly fellow. "Sandford," he said to me one day, "I admire your principles, but you seem to me lamentably deficient in common sense. Now, I've lots of common sense, but my principles are quisby."

WINIFRED: Quisby?

SANDFORD: A Casowary term, my darling, signifying queer. "I take you prisoner, till you've taught me principles and I have taught you common sense!" He did it. Finally, he let me go, but on one condition!

WINIFRED: What?

SANDFORD: Before I sailed, he made me take an oath that I would never again talk in rounded periods.

WINIFRED: Oh, Henry, this accounts for the change in your conversation.

SANDFORD: Isn't it an improvement?

WINIFRED: I like you ever so much better, now that you occasionally use an adjective where a punctilious purity insists upon an adverb.

SANDFORD: But, I say, Winifred, you must drop your rounded periods as well.

WINIFRED: May I?

SANDFORD: You must.

WINIFRED: How jolly!

SANDFORD: I have come to the conclusion that a strictly grammatical
life is not worth living.

DUET.—WINIFRED AND SANDFORD.

SANDFORD: For the future, say I,
    Lindley Murray, good-bye!
  I shall not mind my P's or my Q's!
WINIFRED: I shall not cross my T's,
    And to loop all my E's
  I politely but firmly refuse.
SANDFORD: Disregarding the tense
    I shall talk common sense!
WINIFRED: We never have talked it before!
SANDFORD: Now that once I have seen
    What a prig I have been,
  I won't be a prig any more!
WINIFRED: No, don't!
SANDFORD: I won't!
  I won't be a prig any more!
WINIFRED: Like a mute I won't look!
SANDFORD: I won't talk like a book!
WINIFRED: I'll play you the liveliest tunes!
SANDFORD: For the future, say I,
    Lindley Murray, good-bye!
  Propriety, prisms, and prunes!
BOTH: Propriety, prisms, and prunes!
WINIFRED: You may go to your club
    Take a hand at the rub—
SANDFORD: And you'll think all the better of me;
    For a wife always snubs
    That example to hubs,
  Who always comes home to his tea!
WINIFRED: To the play we will go
    And see every show—
  You will take me to concerts and balls?

SANDFORD: And sometimes you and I—
    In a very black tie—
  Will visit the music halls!
WINIFRED: We will!
SANDFORD: We will!
BOTH: We'll visit the music halls!
WINIFRED: We'll have supper at Scott's
    And of fun we'll have lots!
SANDFORD: Though married, we'll always be spoons!
WINIFRED: For the future, say I,
    Lindley Murray, good-bye!
  Propriety, prisms, and prunes!
BOTH: Propriety, prisms, and prunes!

DANCE

Enter TOMMY MERTON.

TOMMY: Good gracious! Sandford! and flirting with my intended wife!

SANDFORD: His wife! What does he mean?

WINIFRED: Oh, by the bye, I quite forgot to tell you, I am to be married to Tommy this morning.

SANDFORD: Married!

WINIFRED: Believing you had been devoured, I no longer cared what became of me, so I reluctantly consented.

SANDFORD: But you won't marry one another now I have turned up again?

WINIFRED: Are we not engaged?

SANDFORD: Winifred, you raise a very delicate question. A young lady supposes her first fiancé to have been devoured, she becomes affianced to a second fiancé. But her first fiancé has not been devoured. To which of her fiancés is she affianced?

TOMMY: Sandford, you awaken old associations. If it takes two men and a boy two-and-a-half days to build a brick wall, in how many days could three men and three-quarters of a boy—no, I give it up. I was never good at that sort of thing.

SANDFORD: The point requires consideration.

WINIFRED: I will leave it to you to consider it; but whatever you decide, I shan't marry Tommy.

TOMMY: Then I think that decides it.

              SYDNEY GRUNDY AND EDWARD SOLOMON

Trio.—Winifred, Sandford, and Tommy.

Sandford: Just one word before you go,
    Just one more caress!
  Now we are engaged, you know,
    What's one more or less?
Tommy: Oh, you rude behaver!
    Not while I am here.
Winifred: Kissing goes by favour—
Sandford: Don't you interfere. (*Embrace*)
Tommy: Sandford having had his share,
    Give me one as well, (*Seizes* Winifred)
Sandford: This is more than I can bear.
Tommy: Kiss and never tell. (*Kisses* Winifred)
Sanford: Here, I say, young shaver!
Tommy (*to* Winifred): Give me back my own,
    Kissing goes by favour.
Winifred: Leave my lips alone.

Ensemble.

Tommy: Kissing goes by favour,
    Give me back my own.
Win & Sand: Kissing goes by favour.
    Leave my/her lips alone.
Exeunt Sandford *and* Winifred.
Re-enter Vicar.
Vicar: At last I have escaped the widow's clutches.
Tommy: My respected tutor!
Vicar: Here already! You're before your time!
Tommy: Such was my impatience—
Vicar: Oh, pooh, pooh! I have some business matters to attend to
    before the wedding. A most important appointment with Miss Bly.
Tommy: Miss Bly is coming here?
Vicar: Our Society has now been in operation twelve months, and the
    consideration of our first annual report demands immediate attention.
Tommy: Will she be alone?
Vicar: Certainly not. She will be accompanied by the ladies of the
    corps de ballet. There is safety in numbers.

TOMMY: I must inform my groomsmen of this assignation. (*Exit*)

VICAR: By all means. Anything to get rid of him. I find from experience that the harmony of the relations between Church and Stage is always marred by the presence of third persons. Miss Bly! I know her footstep.

Enter NELLY BLY *and* BALLET.

NELLY: Good morning, Vicar.

VICAR: Good morning, Miss Bly.

NELLY: How well you're looking!

VICAR: I was about to make the same remark. But let us to business.

AGATHA: }
CYNTHIA: } Good morning, Vicar.
BLANCHE: }

VICAR: My dear young ladies, excuse me for not greeting you before. Bless me, how remarkably well all of you—but let us to business.

NELLY: Here is my report. (*reads*)—"In presenting their First Annual Report, the committee of the Co-operative Clerical Reform Association regret to announce that the finances are in a deplorable condition. Under these circumstances, it has been unanimously resolved to appeal to the public for subscriptions."

VICAR: A very wise determination.

CYNTHIA: At the same time, I don't quite see what the public has to do with it.

VICAR: My dear child, whenever there's money to be raised the public has everything to do with it. Now don't distress yourself. Leave that to the clergy. Is the clergy are proficient in anything, it is appealing to the public for subscriptions.

BLANCHE: It seems to me, the less the public has to do with it, the better.

VICAR: Decidedly. Let the public find the money, and the less the public has to do with it the better.

NELLY: (*reads*) "The committee also regret that since the inaugural meeting not a single patron of the society (*after having enjoyed the full benefit of the advertisement*) has put in an appearance, with the exception of the Rev. William Barlow, Vicar of Bray."

CHORUS: Bravo! bravo!

NELLY: "Whose assiduous attentions to the ladies of the ballet—"

VICAR: "What's that? Whose assiduous attentions to the ladies of the ballet have been highly appreciated." I don't quite like the way that's put.

AGATHA: What's the matter with it?

VICAR: This is evidently an unsophisticated composition. Have you a pencil? Thank you. "Whose assiduous attentions to the duties of his position cannot be too highly commended."

CHORUS: Hear, hear, hear!

NELLY: "On the vexed question of the length of their skirts, the ballet have consented to a compromise. In consideration of the clergy agreeing to shorten their discourses, the ballet have lengthened their dresses."

VICAR: Humph! I think you've overdone it!

CYNTHIA: It is a matter of taste, Vicar.

VICAR: Alas, we live in a degenerate age. Even the ballet is not what it used to be.

NELLY: Wait till you see our new pas de cinq, and I think you will admit, it is a great improvement.

VICAR: You are rehearsing a new pas de cinq? What is it like?

NELLY: Unfortunately, one of the girls is absent, or we'd show you.

VICAR: Couldn't you find a substitute?

CHORUS: The Vicar! The Vicar!

BLANCHE: Will you join us?

VICAR: Anything I can do to promote a better feeling between Church and Stage I'll do with pleasure. How do I begin?

NELLY: We begin. You stand doing this.

VICAR: Oh! I stand doing that? I see.

NELLY: Well, do it.

VICAR: I shall be rather clumsy at first.

NELLY: Now, off! Now, cross to me! Now, do as I do! Very good indeed!

VICAR: Oh! I shall soon get used to it.

NELLY: Ladies, begin!

DANCE.

Exeunt.

Re-enter TOMMY MERTON *and* CHORUS *of* HUNTSMEN.

TOMMY: My friends, I have to inform you of a slight modification in the bridal arrangements. There will be no bride.

CHORUS: No bride!

TOMMY: At the last moment Miss Barlow has thrown me over. I may observe, you all know what it is to be thrown over.

1st Huntsman: What has caused this cropper?

Tommy: The unexpected arrival of our old friend, Sandford.

Chorus: Sandford!

1st Huntsman: I thought he was devoured.

Tommy: On the contrary, he was never better in his life.

1st Huntsman: No wonder you're annoyed.

Tommy: But I'm not annoyed. I'm overjoyed. Perceive my paradoxical position.

Concerted Piece.—Tommy, Rowe, and Huntsmen.

Tommy: I am not so much vexed
      As puzzled and perplexed;
    My quandary is curiously curious.
      Here I am overjoyed,
      When I should feel annoyed—
    In fact I should feel frantically furious.
      In this dilemma, who
      Can counsel me but you?
    In no one is my confidence impliciter,
      To whom am I to go?

Enter Rowe.

Chorus: To Mr. Bedford Rowe!

Rowe: Your confidential family Solicitor!

Tommy & Chorus: Your coming, Mr. Rowe,
      Is very a propos;
    In no one is our confidence impliciter
      To whom am I/is he to go,
      If not to Mr. Rowe?

Rowe: Your confidential family Solicitor!

Tommy: Undoubtedly, his charge
      Is very much too large—

Rowe: A parsimony paltry and penurious,
      In legal matters is
      The worst of policies,
    As injudicious as it is injurious.

Tommy: You mean, take your advice
      And never mind the price?

Rowe: My meaning, Sir, could not be well expliciter,

TOMMY: You mean I ought to go
  To Mr. Bedford Rowe
ROWE: Your confidential family Solicitor!
MERTON & CHORUS: Oh never mind the price
  But act on your/his advice
 In no one is my/our confidence impliciter
  To whom am I/is he to go,
  If not to Mr. Rowe?
ROWE: Your confidential family Solicitor!
ROWE: Gentlemen, I cannot fail to be deeply touched by this proof of
 your esteem, but I must consider the interests of my other clients.
TOMMY: What are those?
ROWE: Writs! As the confidential family solicitor of the ladies of the
 corps de ballet I have issued thirteen of them, of which as your
 confidential family solicitor I have accepted service, in thirteen
 actions of breach of promise of marriage.
CHORUS: Phew!
ROWE: This is a serious matter. You must be aware that you have
 trifled with their young affections.
TOMMY: Then it's a trifling matter.
ROWE: Mr. Merton, as a private friend, I appreciate your wit and
 humour, but in my professional capacity it is my duty to warn you
 that a heartless and unseemly levity will only aggravate the damages.
TOMMY: Then what would you advise?
ROWE: Your only course is to compromise the actions.
TOMMY: How?
ROWE: By marrying the young ladies.
TOMMY: But we are all engaged to the lady-teachers. If we throw them
 over, can't they all bring actions?
ROWE: As their confidential family solicitor, I shall certainly advise
 them to pursue that course.
TOMMY: Then it makes no difference which of them we marry?
ROWE: To your confidential family solicitor, no difference whatever.
TOMMY: Groomsmen, what say you? You have been engaged to each,
 which do you prefer?
CHORUS: The ballet!
ROWE: Then I will call my clients!
Exit.
Enter CHORUS *of* LADIES *of the* BALLET.

Chorus of Corps De Ballet.

We no longer gyrate;
Measures much more sedate
Better suit the estate
Of the unfortunate.
    Our diversion
    In desertion
Is a slide and a hop;
    Aggravating
    Is rotating,
So we stop, and we flop.

TOMMY: Ladies, we have seen the error of our ways, and we have come back penitent.

NELLY: Oh, that's all very well, but will you marry us?

TOMMY: If you will settle the actions.

NELLY: We must be settled first.

TOMMY: You shall be. You were our first loves, and you shall be our first wives. Seal the contract.

Re-enter CHORUS *of* TEACHERS *and* CHORUS *of* STUDENTS *severally.*

CONCERTED PIECE.—TEACHERS, STUDENTS, HUNTSMEN, and
CORPS DE BALLET.

AGATHA: See!

JOHN: See!

TEACHERS: We saw!

STUDENTS: We saw!

ALL: A kiss!

TEACHERS: With other girls they dally

BALLET: We're no more girls than you are, miss.

TEACHERS: We will no longer suffer this

BALLET: We're ladies of the ballet.

HUNTSMEN: We much prefer the ballet

TEACHERS: We will no longer suffer this,

ALL: They much prefer the ballet.

STUDENTS (*to* TEACHERS): Oh give us back our peace of mind
    We'll marry you if you'll be kind.

TEACHERS: But you are High,

If we comply—
STUDENTS: High we'll be no more!
    We will be Low!
    Oh, ladies, oh!
  Hear us, we implore!
HUNTSMEN: Do, ladies, do!
BALLET: For it is too
  Good a chance to miss.
HUNTSMEN & BALLET: Too good a chance to miss.
TEACHERS & HUNTSMEN: Rise, students, rise,
      Our/Their heart replies
ALL: Yes, beloved, yes!
Enter CHILDREN.

CHORUS OF CHILDREN

Lucky little boys and girls of Bray!
We have got another holiday!
Merrily we skip and merrily we hop—
Oranges and nuts and ginger pop!
Bread and jam for breakfast, marmalade for tea!
Lucky little boys and girls are we!

Lucky little boys and girls of Bray!
Teacher, she is going to be wed today!
Tommy Merton's promised us a slice of cake!
Tommy is a brick, and no mistake!
When the cake is eaten, won't we have a spree?
Lucky little boys and girls are we!

Re-enter VICAR *with* WINIFRED.

WEDDING CHORUS and PROCESSION.
CHILDREN, TEACHERS, BALLET, HUNTSMEN, STUDENTS.

Lady fair,
    We come to meet thee,
        Upon this thy wedding day!
Lady fair,
    We come to greet thee,

And with flowers strew the way!
Ring out, bells, cheerily! Ring out, unwearily!
    Ring out your jubilant message again!
Carol, bells, merrily! Telling us, verily,
    Life has its pleasure as well as its pain!
        Ring out, ring out, ring out!

Enter SANDFORD.

SANDFORD: Halt!

VICAR: What is this? Who has the impudence—

SANDFORD: Don't you all recognise me?

OMNES: Sandford!

VICAR: Oh, there's some mistake! Sandford was eaten and digested long ago.

SANDFORD: I am not eaten, and I claim my bride.

VICAR: Your bride indeed! I beg your pardon, sir! My daughter us about to be married to Thomas Merton, of Bray Manor, Esquire.

SANDFORD: I dispute that assertion.

VICAR: You'd dispute anything. I put it to any impartial person—

SANDFORD: Will you put it to Winifred?

Re-enter MRS. MERTON.

VICAR: Oh, stuff and nonsense, to the Church proceed!

Re-enter ROWE.

ROWE: Stop! I injunct you, Barlow!

VICAR: More obstruction!

ROWE: As the confidential family solicitor of two of your scandalised parishioners, it becomes my painful duty to serve you with this inhibition.

VICAR: Oh, I'm inhibited, am I? Pray, what for?

ROWE: For your notorious ritualistic practices.

VICAR: Now, Rowe, old fellow, I don't call this kind. Wasn't it by your advice that I turned High?

ROWE: Yes, but you turned too High. In fact, you've got quite gamey. And to make matters worse, the Court of Arches has this day deprived you of your benefice, and in consideration of his missionary labours has appointed the Rev. Henry Sandford, Vicar of Bray.

SANDFORD: Me?

OMNES: Sandford!

VICAR: That's all nonsense. The Court of Arches has no power to do anything of the sort.

Rowe: My dear sir, it's done it. It isn't the first time the Court of Arches has exceeded its jurisdiction.

Vicar: Can't I appeal?

Rowe: Oh, yes, you can appeal.

Vicar: Then I'll appeal.

Rowe: But if you want to win, I should advise you to turn Low again.

Vicar: Then I'll turn Low. Vicar of Bray I am, and Vicar of Bray I mean to be, whatever happens.

Sandford: But how do you propose to deal with my pretensions?

Tommy: And am I to be utterly ignored?

Vicar: I'll soon settle you! Look here, resign your claim and I consent to your marriage with Winifred.

Mrs. M.: (*to* Tommy) Then you can marry Nelly.

Vicar: You consent?

Sandford: On one condition—that you will be Low once more.

Rowe: Oh, that's quite understood.

Vicar: I will be Lower than ever.

Finale.

Mrs. M.: Oh, William, sweet William, since Low you will be,
     There's nothing to hinder you marrying me!

Vicar: My dearest Matilda, that's perfectly true.

Mrs. M.: (*coaxingly*) Oh come to the arms that are waiting for you,

Vicar: Well I think that's about the best thing I can do.

All: I think that's about the best thing you can do.

Chorus: Hurray! hurray! hurray!
    He always makes it pay
      With heart and voice
      Let all rejoice
    He's Vicar still of Bray!
    And now this merry May morning
      Uniting our voices, we pray
    Long live he, his office adorning!
      All hail to the Vicar of Bray!

End of Opera.

The libretto has the following finale.

Mrs. M.: Oh, William, sweet William, since Low you will be,
    There's nothing to hinder you marrying me!

Vicar: My dearest Matilda, that's perfectly true.

Mrs. M.: Oh come to the arms that are waiting for you,

Vicar: I think that's about the best thing I can do.

Chorus: I think that's about the best thing you can do.

Rowe: And if when you're married, you find it a bore—

Chorus: N.B. the Jackson case!

Rowe: You can easily show one another the door—

Chorus: E.G. the Jackson case!

Mrs. M.: But William will never kick over the trace—

Chorus: Pooh, pooh, the Jackson case!

Vicar: The living of Bray I will never disgrace!

Chorus: Bad, bad old Jackson case!

Vicar: We'll prove love still lingers—

Mrs. M.: And gaily our fingers—

Both: We'll snap in the face of the Jackson case!

Chorus: They'll snap in the face of the Jackson case!

And now this merry May morning

Uniting our voices, we pray—

Children: Long live he, his office adorning!

Omnes: All hail to the Vicar of Bray!

Curtain.

bookfinity™

Discover more of your favorite classics with Bookfinity™.

- Track your reading with custom book lists.
- Get great book recommendations for your personalized Reader Type.
- Add reviews for your favorite books.
- AND MUCH MORE!

Visit **bookfinity.com** and take the fun Reader Type quiz to get started.

Enjoy our classic and modern companion pairings!

Classic & Modern